The Colors of Life

by

Kevin Maddock

DORRANCE
PUBLISHING CO
EST. 1920
PITTSBURGH, PENNSYLVANIA 15238

Dorrance Publishing Co
585 Alpha Drive
Pittsburgh, PA 15238
Visit our website at www.dorrancebookstore.com

ISBN: 978-1-6491-3240-6
eISBN: 978-1-6491-3716-6

A Second Chance

I look out and see the dark night.
I see the moon as it reflects the light,
And the stars that twinkle so bright.

I hear the rain as it calms my sleeping eyes,
And the thunder that wakes me up with surprise.
I hear the birds chirping so loud,
And the crickets playing to an endless crowd.

The colors and sounds—it's all so right.
I'm glad I never met that endless night.
Because of frightful pain and mindless bliss,
I may have forever missed sweet Earth's kiss.

But now I have a Second Chance,
To take a wonderful and second glance.
I'm now saying it in a sure way.
Thank you, sweet Lord, for another day.

Current Times

Thinking of life.
The mind going to the past.
The pictures flickering by so fast.

Why does the mind only think of the past?
Why not—the now or the future?
A scary thought turning into a blur.

Current times—you're unable to explain.
The daily thought of trying to get through.
Fighting against that color of blue.

Why not the times of the future ahead?
Do the times of the past cloud your mind?
Is the future too hard to find?

A future that I hope is there.
A current time that I will fight through.
A past that makes me realize the color of blue.

My past has built the foundations of my life ahead.
It's helped me with all the colors that may come.
The colors that may be blind to some,
Are the same I have while dreaming in bed.

My Mind

My mind thinks in colors.
Emotional colors that all come through.
The same colors that affect you.

My mind thinks in numbers.
Signs and symbols reflecting my thought.
Equations never filling that empty spot.

It's a mind that's no different than you—
Colors of red, white, green or blue.
It's a mind of vivid dreams—
At times on its own, or so it seems.

I can think of the past and all that I had.
The times of wonder and the times of bad.
The past that gave me a wonderful life.
The colors leading me through a normal strife.

The future is still to come.
What is my mind thinking?
Numbers and colors—that's what I say.
The true thought is another day.

Brennen's Eyes

If my eyes could see—
See like the eyes of Brennen.
What would they see?
Would they even see me?

The eyes of wonder—
Nothing to fear;
But everything to fret.
Eyes that never forget.

Eyes that can hear and smell.
Eyes that can give and tell.
Eyes that never yell.

What do they see?
What do they hear?
Why the brilliant glare?

Is the gift that he doesn't see?
Is the gift that he sees more than me?
I wish he could see.
I wish he could see me.

Turns

We may love—we may weep.
Life takes us on turns.

Turns that make us wonder.
Turns that make us think.
We wonder about the turns.
We may fight—we may sleep.
Thinking about what we wondered.

Simple is what we ask for,
But then simple is what we ignore.
Simple—like the flowers growing along a walk,
While our eyes still turn and baulk.

We turn away with eyes aside—
Not even seeing the other side.
Bushes to the left and bushes to the right.
We may miss that Spring flower growing upright.

We all mature and things turn blue.
The shadows and the Angels try to come through.
Some things that are older can turn out to be new,
And some of the turns can turn out to be true.

The Person That Is Me

Someday, I'll be perfect.
That time I'll wait to see.
I'll settle for now—the person that is me.

I try to please.
I see the failing in that.
Like a Winter's breeze.
The wind blowing the hat.

A robot—I've been called, that's true.
I'm not a robot and that I know.
I'm a person still needing to grow.

I'm not perfect, and I'll never be.
Some things, I don't think you can see.
I'll always have my dreams with you and me.
The dreams that come with life.

Our mutual times of strife.
Memories from the time in the past.
Memories yet to be cast.

Someday, I'll be perfect.
Until that time
I'm hoping for the perfect memories that can be.

The Older I Get

The older I get—
Some things come true.
Some are red and some are blue.
It's hard to let the colors come through.

The older I get—
The time goes so fast.
It's hard to keep up with my growing past.
Like a sailboat missing its mast.

Some friends have come and gone.
Some family, too.
I look back and forth.
And wonder—what I am to do.

The question may be—not what to do,
Or what should I have done.
My bad mistakes make me blue,
And some of my red mistakes were fun to do.

The older I get—
I'm still wondering what to do.
To live in the past or the new.

The NEW scares me—I must admit.

The problems of life seem to grow.

I'm worried about that new low.

The older I get—

It doesn't seem much fun.

But I promise to stay in this World—

Till Jesus tells me I'm done.

Winter

Snow piling up to block my way.
Frigid temps making me blue.
I'm waiting for that first Spring day.

Winter, I admit, is my time of dislike.
The cold and the slush—I'm not a fan.
It's time for Winter to take a hike.

Counting down to the start of Spring.
Clearing the blue and bringing in the green.
Hearing the Song Birds beginning to sing.
A better picture to be seen.

The Towers

I watched the sky after that day.
Not a thing to see.
All the planes being held at bay.

I remember crying to the Towers coming down.
Hours of TV watching those scenes.
A World realizing a terrorist clown.

Thousands lost of all race and creed.
A coward's way to make a point.
A day when the World did bleed.

We had support after that day.
Every country shed their tears.
All the World showed their fears.
Today it's gone—I admit in some way.

The Towers are gone and the years have went.
The lives lost and the memories spent.
The Child's life with an empty spot.
The empty mind with nothing sought.

There's a new Tower there—so they say.
And a memory of the ones we lost.
Will we always remember those buildings' cost?
No matter what—God Bless the U.S.A.

What Is Life

What is life?
Living for another day.
Fighting through the daily strife.
Closing your eyes and finding that way.

Emotions making that life's grind.
The colors showing our life's mind.
The love, family and past that we had.
The sorrows, loss and problems that are sad.

Life is a gift—given to me.
A future still yet to see.
There will be good, and there will be bad.
More time to become who I shall be.

If I leave this Earth tomorrow.
I'll leave with a good start.
I'll leave with a thankful heart.
I will leave with no time to borrow.

A Mother Lost

After a horrible loss.
The days and months all see the same.
The combination of grass and moss.
A mind keeps laying that endless blame.

A Mother that left too soon for all.
Caring for us to the end.
Never caring for her final call.
Only worrying about how we will mend.

The memories will never leave my brain.
I'll always remember her style.
Any card game was her gain.
Taking our money—with that laughing smile.

Everyone is remembered from their past.
None are perfect, I do believe.
Sometimes, however, a bronze is cast
For that perfect person God did receive.

The Color of Blue

The color of blue.
The darkest that I've ever gone through.
An emotional color making me sad.
Troubling seas these past weeks—that I've had.

A Father lost years ago.
Xavier and Bengals were his favorite shows.
Times of happiness and times of sad.
I still remember all those times we had.

Now a Mother that's gone too soon.
My eyes staring up to the skies and the moon.
My mind asking the question of why.
No answer coming from that dark night's sky.

Living for others—that was her life.
Even during times of that blue strife.
She worried about your life and your needs.

She cried when I did my wrong.
She forgave me and made me strong.
She's now in the stars—a shining blue.

In the white shimming blue.
I can see it in my eyes.
I will always look up to those skies—
And say, "Mom—I miss you."

Magic Key

If you could see into the future—
What would you see?
Would you see a good life yet to be?
Are you holding in your hand that magic key?

Do you see a life of living in the past?
Are you holding on to that Pharaoh's mast?
Do you picture a better day—
Where the past just goes away?

The future is hard to see.
The past and present may stop the thought.
The future is there for me.
The future will tell me some day—what it has brought.

The problems of life will always be there.
The good times in life will happen, too.
Staying strong will get me through—
So I can enjoy those future good times with you.

If I could see into the future,
What would I see?
I would see a wonderful life ahead of me.
I hope to have that magic key.

Future Dreams

I hate flying, but I want to fly so high.
I want to aim for that beautiful blue.
The blue that is that sky.
A journey to make our life true.

Detours changing our paths.
Challenges blocking the way.
Life lessons learned by the day.
Words written for me to say.

It's our life—let's have fun.
Let's take that graceful run.
An open field with bales of hay.
Future dreams to make our day.

The bushes are still left and right.
I'm still keeping our dreams in sight.
The kite colors are showing so bright.
Let's take that kite to another height.

Parents

A Father that finished every Christmas with words to family.
"You never know when your family will be gone," he said.
I remember the words while laying my head to bed.

A Mother that gave herself to all.
A caring remembered till the end of day.
A future card game yet to play.

Our parents made us who we are.
We aren't perfect and will never be.
Our mistakes in life leaving its scar.
Still given the life ahead to see.

Thinking about my parents—both gone today.
How they did it—I do not know.
Secrets gone, I'm afraid to say.
Imagining both in that wonderful glow.

I miss all the games of the past.
The quarters taken with the winning laugh.
Passing the Ace to a fearful cast.
Hours of talking about the Bengals' staff.

A Father and Mother gone way to soon.
Only memories left to lead my way.
I'm looking at that man on the Moon.
I love what you gave me, and I'll see you some day.

Stages of Life

Of course you are born with nothing to care.
Then at age two—terrible, they say.
Making your parents wanting to pray.

Elementary years take the stage.
The building blocks of life—starting to grow.
Friends for life—you're beginning to know.

High school and the teens coming so quick.
Trying to discover the colors in yourself.
Unable to put your emotions on that shelf.

20s—the start of the adult in you.
The world seems to be well in sight.
Not knowing the truth of starting that fight.

30s—the start in the age of you.
While remembering the past, your future is the next step.
Hoping you had the perfect life's prep.

40s—years have passed and what did I do?
The emotional colors have painted me by now.
I'm not ready for that ending bow.

I think about going back to that elementary life.

Erasing the bad colors that strain my mind.

Replacing them with the good that I can find.

Life is life—that's all I can say.

I've loved the good and will take the bad.

Thank you, Lord, for the Life that I have had.

And I will continue for another day.

Lonely

Lonely—I shouldn't be.
Am I riding a ship on that troubled sea,
Or hanging on to that hopeful thought?

Boredom—a thoughtless mind.
Is it trouble I'm trying to find?

The bushes to the right have started to die.
The dull colors—anyone can see.
Sometimes the wonder of a big sigh.
What is the future going to be?

Placid waters would be my dream.
Imagining those waters in life with you.
A sea turned into a calm of blue.
A troubled mind hunting for the true.

Life of the Past

The life of the past.
The memories coming through.
The future being cast.
The future—I don't know.

My parents' friends—having fun in the night.
Camping, picnics and family fun.
Always laughter within my sight.
A calming night when the day was done.

Some have gone onto that sleep.
Their past will keep my memories alive.
The colors in my mind, I will keep
Until the day that I arrive.

Christmas Past

It's that time of year again—a time of Christmas joy.
A glimmering in the eyes of every girl and boy.
A lifetime of memories—never to forget.

It's those memories that I dearly miss.
Family is gone and traditions lost.
A father always warning of that future cost.

I cry for my Father and Mother that have gone.
Grandparents and others that have all moved on.
The future is here, and it's not the same.

The present is here, and it is today.
Enjoying Christmas with loved ones around—
While still missing that past Christmas sound.

Times have changed—and I miss them much.
A boyhood home gone—and all the such.
The missing of the past—increasing the color of blue.

I believe they are looking from above.
They want us to always remember Christmas past—
But they want us to carry on the future that they have cast.

They're watching over us like a beautiful Dove.

Above the skies with tears of love.

Looking down and wanting to say.

Never forget each Christmas Day.

Happy Holidays. Merry Christmas. Prayers to all.

Facebook Shame

Christmas is coming.
It doesn't seem the same, I know.
Another year
But a year of complete change.

No Mother and Father.
No gifts to exchange.
The problems now increased.
Words of Facebook shame.

The memories will always come back.
The times of change can move that clock.
I admit that nothing will be the same.
Too many reasons to place the blame.

Today is now and the future is ahead.
The past, I admit, will always stay in my mind.
Memories of family—making that bind.
Dreaming of Christmas past, while laying in my bed.

We have a chance to show our strength.
Building on our future and remembering their life.
The fighting and things that need to stop.
Imagine them seeing the current life's strife.

Remember all that we have had.

Remember all the good and the bad.

Think about those past gifts on Christmas Day.

And remember what Dad always had to say.

Evils in Life

The World of today.
Religions on attack.
Mine is better—so they say.
Emotions drawn into that mind of black.

We all live, and we all die.
Troubles of life—they find us all.
Evils in life—making the Angels cry.
Shadows of horror making you crawl.

People lost with no care in sight.
No care for a peaceful mind.
No concern for the human blight.
Not a care for human kind.

Will we wake up and join that fight?
The future is yet ahead to see.
The mindful thought of the human plight.
What is our World coming to be?

Days of Yesterday

The days of yesterday are lost in thought.
The days of tomorrow are not yet brought.
The time of now is the today.

A time of problems—a time to pray.
A time for all to stand up and say.
We're not standing with the problems we got.

People killed because of belief.
Families living in the blue of the grief.
Colors filling the endless mind.

The colors that we all should see.
The colors making us—you and me.
The colors of life—are beautiful to be.

Things

I must admit that I've been through some things.
Some things that make me who I am today.
Is it a World that puts me on an Eagle's wings?
It is a World keeping me from what I should say?

I said I liked that second chance.
I said I like that other glance.
You say that I do not know.
Have you forgot about my time below?

We all have problems and times of doubt.
We wonder what it's all about.
It's normal to wonder and shout.
If only we could have a forward scout.

An answer? I don't think is there.
A better feeling? Is only up to you.
If we all know it, we would share.
Then nobody would go through the color of blue.

Blue is not easy to get through.
It makes it harder to take a stand.
In fact, it makes it harder to understand.
However, clearing the blue is needed for you.

I wish I could have the magic answer.
The answer that hasn't come to me.
The answer that I'm yet to see.

I dream of a perfect time.
A time where you don't need to know.
A time of a perfect glow.

Tears

How do you explain the tears?
Not of joy—nor of pain.
How do you explain the years?
The stories of the past and the current of mundane.

Thinking about my childhood past.
Color not yet filling my mind.
Life not yet completing that cast.
An open mind as if it were blind.

Years say the childhood is gone.
I refuse to let that go.
Some say—Father Time has won.
I refuse to take that blow.

My tears—I cannot explain.
I'm thinking of the future and maybe the past.
I admit, I don't like the plain.
Even with the tears, I want my years to last.

The Pain

Even though I'm a guy, I admit that I sit here and cry at night.
I shield my eyes and shade the light.
I wonder how to fight the fight.

I know the pain that we all have.
I fight the pain that is with me.
The pain that we all see.
The current pain making me be.

Tomorrow's not promised—so they say.
Tomorrow is just another day.
A day to see the other side.
Hoping to keep a little pride.

Fighting to keep that daily day.
Ignoring the strife and wanting to stay.
The mind wondering in a wonderous way.
The same mind making the need to pray.

Never to be that perfect friend.
Never to be that perfect husband.
I'll never be that perfect guy.
Once again, I'm making me cry.

I am who I am.

That's all I am.

I am who I will be.

That's all I can see.

Life's Grind

Sometimes—I don't shed that tear.
I may not show the emotion you want.
I may not show the wonder of fear.
Like fans waiting for that glorious stunt.

I keep it in, that I admit.
It is there—I admit, too.
Held by the times of grit.
Held by the colors of blue.

My tears are wet—yes, they are.
A taste of salt upon my cheeks.
Memories of the past times gone so far.
The aging of the future coming in weeks.

I close my mind and look ahead.
I shadow those eyes from the dread.
Keeping the future thought in my mind.
I'm not stopping that living grind.

Getting Older

It's funny how we look at age through the years.
At times, we want to speed it up
Other times, we want to slow it down.
Time may not be what it appears.

There's the time of being a kid.
The World is your playground—or so they say.
No Demons yet for you to rid.
The day is meant for you to play.

Then comes high school and graduation day.
A day of looking to the future and the promise ahead.
Some thoughts and worries are in the way—
But you still sleep soundly in your bed.

Early adult—it's hard to explain.
The future's ahead while the past is still today.
Some of the mistakes have left their stain.
While some of the past—you'd like to get away.

Middle age—the time I'm in now.
Can I slow that age clock that I've yearned?
Can I do good and take a bow?
Can I relax and take the time that I've earned?

Now's a time for time to slow.

The slides and pictures make a perfect show.

You think about the past more than the new.

You're sometimes afraid of what's coming to you.

Old age is something I don't know.

Will I want the clock to speed or slow?

Will my time be good or bad?

Hopefully, my future won't make me sad.

That age clock—I know is part of life.

Demons and Angels are with us all.

We all have that human strife.

But I want to slow that clock down before my final call.

I Promise

Waiting for news while the butterflies fly.
A mind staying in the color of blue.
Prince is gone, and we wonder why?
My mind is back with no clue.

I often think of that final night.
I worry for those I leave behind.
Never stopping that daily fight.
The colors of life—a normal grind.

I'm thinking too much—that I know.
Anything can happen—that I'll say.
I'll use this—and try to grow.
This I promise, and say today.

The Anger of Life

The grey side that comes through.
A mind thinking too much.
The head wondering too blue.

Wondering about the problems of today.
Thinking about the problems of tomorrow.
Words in my mind about what to say.

Calming down my mind's sorrow.
We all have our problems and thought.
We all have a different strife.

The anger of the life we got.
We ignore how God's made our life right.

If I Met the Lord Tonight

If I went to see the Lord tonight,
would I leave behind a meaningful life?
Are my footsteps upon that ground?
Will my memories stay around?

I wonder if you'll remember me.
Will the memories be good or bad?
It's hard to imagine what you would see.
It's hard to look back at the life I had.

A Facebook life of the pictured past.
A hidden message in the post you like.
Mindless thoughts shown with the keys that I strike.
Pictures and time, they go so fast.

A Second Chance was given to me.
Actually, I've been given more than three.
Whether three or four—what did I give?
What have I done with the life that I live?

I'm not perfect—I do admit.
I've ignored chances and taken the other way.
I've stood up when I should sit—
And I've not made the best of every day.

So if I met the Lord tonight—
I hope he would forgive my human plight.
I'd show him my love for my family, friends and wife.
I would thank him for a wonderful life.

When Life Gets You Down

When life gets you down
What do you do?
When life gets you down
How do you get through?

Can I make it through?
Can I even last another day by day?
Can I trust in you?
Can I make it through another day?

Believe me, I want to fight,
There's no more time for me to borrow.
Even with the shadows blocking my sight,
I really want to see you tomorrow.

Changing the Blue

My mind thinks in different ways.
The colors that you may not see.
The hidden dangers of a blue sea.

Hidden waves wondering around.
Waves rocking our emotional ship.
Staying away from that possible tip.

Changing the blue is what I'll do.
I'll promise to change that color to new.
Taking away that color of blue.

That Candle

I'm sitting here wondering about the life of tonight.
A wedding down and one yet to come.
Does the pain, however, cloud my hopeful sight?

I'm feeling useless at times, I must admit.
I'm wondering how to get it fixed.
I'm wanting to get that candle relit.

That candle that showed the colors.
Blue, red, green and yellow.
A candle that could even show me the mellow.

I want it back—that candle in me.
I want it back so you can see.
That candle is what I used to be.

That Old Time

That old time—when you had to say it face to face.
At least on a phone, you told them with a voice.
Today's world is a different place.

Throwing it on the Web is not a good place for me.
Why show it for all of Facebook to see?
You're mind shaming—like it's the true life.
You're mind building a family's strife.

That old time when you would write a letter.
Words written instead of a splatter.
The old times seem so much better.

Pieces of metal thrown out like knives.
Mental edges cutting real deep.
Words not understood by all.
A family tumbling into a Facebook fall.

I'm wishing for healing that all I love.
Taking out the mindless blue of clutter.
Dreaming about our common Angels above.

Problems

The grey side that comes through.
A mind thinking too much.
The head wondering too blue.

Wondering about the problems of today.
Thinking about the problems of tomorrow.
Words in my mind about what to say.
Calming down my mind's sorrow.

We all have our problems and thought.
We all have a different strife.
The anger of the life we got.
We ignore how God's made our life right.

Problems of Age

If I'm not around in 6 months—
I'll say I tried my best.
Hoping my problems are put to rest.

Remembering the past and all I had.
The family gathering all around.
The people talking, such a beautiful sound.

Kids today—that have grown up.
Taking their spot upon that stage.
Not yet to realize the problems of age.

The color of blue still comes through.
The happy color seems to be rare.
I close my eyes—and it is there.

When I see the Lord sometime.
I hope the bad colors will be washed away.
I hope to see that other day.

When I pass, I will say
I hope they forgive the bad in me.
Just imagine the good—that Good could see.

Loss of a Friend

You have left us now.
A time too soon.
Too early to take that final bow.

A perfect grin taken away.
A certain laughter that would make my day.
It's hard to believe that's all gone today.

Memories are now all we have.
The times of fun and games in the past.
The memories that have been cast.

You have left us now.
That is hard to know.
My heart's hurting deep below.

RIP, Brian McHugh.

Shades of Blue

The shades of blue—
The things I can't get through.
The Jimmy Hendrix playing—
I wonder about the things I'm saying.

I've talked about a Second Chance.
I've even taken a second stance.
The colors in my thoughts are all abound—
While my poems try to take a look around.

Red, yellow, green and grey—
These are the colors that tell what I say.
Me being laid back and just feeling the day-by-day—
Does not make the pain go away.

Some colors may come through to be sad.
I know there's much life to be had.
I'm still waiting for the good that may come.
Even if not me, it may happen to some.

Don't take that wrong.
I love my life.
I love my wife.
I actually still feel strong.

This is about emotions.

The emotions we all have and want to hide.

This is about emotions.

The emotions we all have that show our side.

Emotions are the feelings that make us who we are.

They are the thoughts that shape our mortal being.

They can hinder or take us very far.

They can also close our eyes from the needed seeing.

Destination

Where will my destination be?
What will happen at the end of me?
Will I go up to see the sky's light?
Or will I see that forever night?

I'm hoping the crickets keep playing.
Playing to that endless crowd.
My face showing in that beautiful cloud.

I'm hoping that you remember me.
Living the only way I know how.
Living the Colors of Life before making that bow.

That destination will be.
It's in a higher hand—more than me.
Someday—I'll give up that fight.
Someday—I'll see that light.